She Stood For
FREEDOM

"You can't make a difference by doing nothing."
—Joan Trumpauer Mulholland

Photograph on page 14, courtesy of the Birmingham Civil Rights Institute (BCRI). Used by permission.

Illustration on pages 20 and 21 based on the original photograph by Fred Blackwell. Used by permission.

Photographs on pages 24 and 25, courtesy of Matt Herron. Used by permission.

Visit us at ShadowMountain.com

Library of Congress Cataloging-in-Publication Data

Names: Mulholland, Loki, author. | Fairwell, Angela, author. | Janssen, Charlotta, illustrator.

Title: She stood for freedom : the untold story of a civil rights hero, Joan Trumpauer Mulholland / Loki Mulholland and Angela Fairwell; illustrated by Charlotta Janssen.

Description: Salt Lake City, Utah : Shadow Mountain, [2016] | ?2016

Identifiers: LCCN 2015041340 | ISBN 9781629721767 (hardbound : alk. paper)

Subjects: LCSH: Mulholland, Joan Trumpauer, 1941– | Women civil rights Workers—United States—Biography. | Civil rights movements—United States—History—20th century. | African Americans—Civil Rights—History—20th century.

Classification: LCC JC599.U5 M85 2016 | DDC 323.092—dc23

Printed in China   3/2016
RR Donnelley, Shenzhen China

10 9 8 7 6 5 4 3 2 1

SHE STOOD FOR FREEDOM

The Untold Story of a Civil Rights Hero,

JOAN TRUMPAUER MULHOLLAND

LOKI MULHOLLAND and ANGELA FAIRWELL
Illustrated by CHARLOTTA JANSSEN

SHADOW
MOUNTAIN

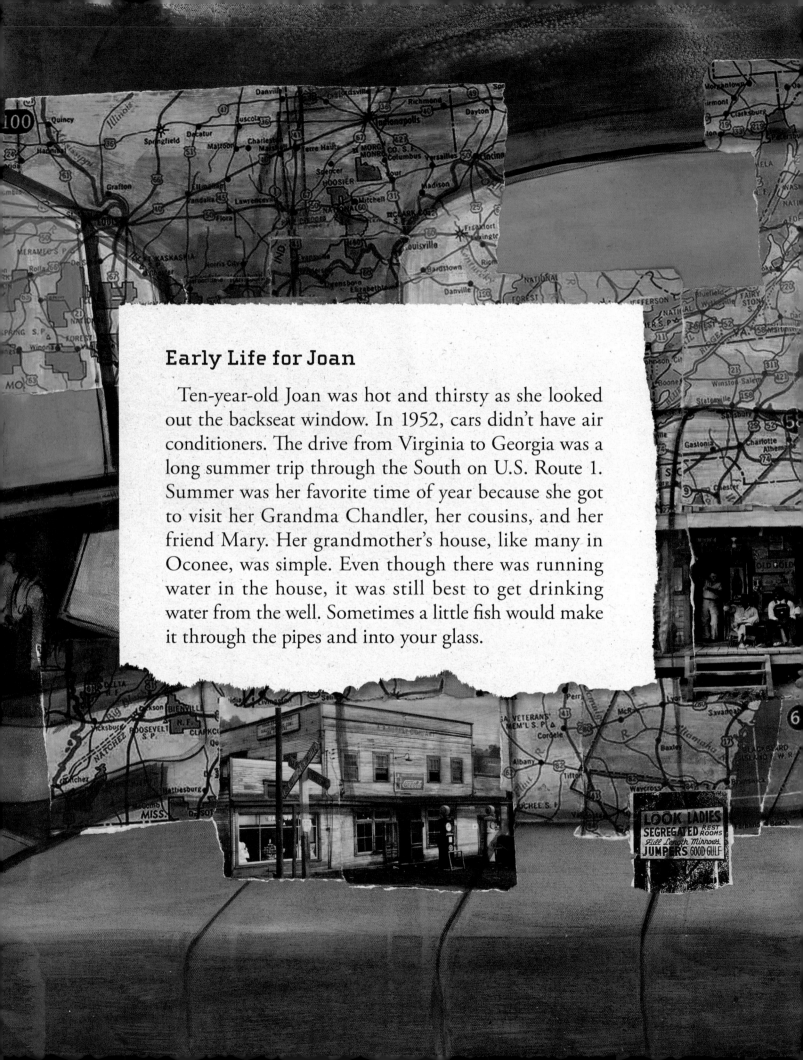

Early Life for Joan

Ten-year-old Joan was hot and thirsty as she looked out the backseat window. In 1952, cars didn't have air conditioners. The drive from Virginia to Georgia was a long summer trip through the South on U.S. Route 1. Summer was her favorite time of year because she got to visit her Grandma Chandler, her cousins, and her friend Mary. Her grandmother's house, like many in Oconee, was simple. Even though there was running water in the house, it was still best to get drinking water from the well. Sometimes a little fish would make it through the pipes and into your glass.

Life in the South

Joan grew up in Arlington, Virginia, at a time when there was a lot of discrimination and hatred against blacks. They weren't allowed to eat at the same lunch counter, sit in the same part of the bus, or go to the same school. Segregated bathrooms at gas stations and stores were part of everyday life. It was even against the law for whites and blacks to worship together. That was just life in the South.

In church, Joan was taught that God loved all of His children (no matter the color of their skin) and that we should treat each other the way we wanted to be treated.

In school, Joan's class stood at attention to sing "Dixie," and she memorized the Declaration of Independence, which says "All men are created equal."

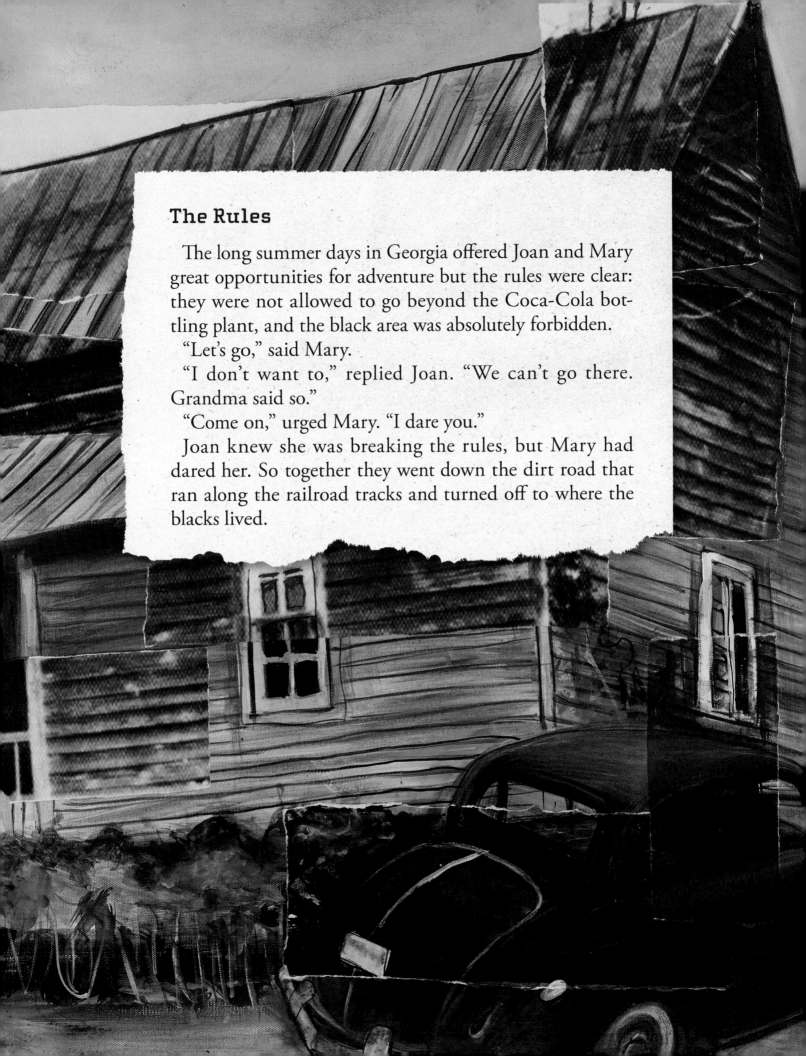

The Rules

The long summer days in Georgia offered Joan and Mary great opportunities for adventure but the rules were clear: they were not allowed to go beyond the Coca-Cola bottling plant, and the black area was absolutely forbidden.

"Let's go," said Mary.

"I don't want to," replied Joan. "We can't go there. Grandma said so."

"Come on," urged Mary. "I dare you."

Joan knew she was breaking the rules, but Mary had dared her. So together they went down the dirt road that ran along the railroad tracks and turned off to where the blacks lived.

The Schoolhouse

Joan's grandmother was poor, but not as poor as the blacks in Oconee.

"I think the people here are afraid of us," Joan whispered to Mary. She thought it was strange that no one wanted to be seen anywhere near them and hid themselves behind their houses and doors.

When Joan and Mary reached the black schoolhouse, Joan stopped and stared. It was not like the brand-new brick school for the white children.

This was a one-room shack on stone piles with a stove in the middle for warmth.

Joan's soul was rattled. This was not fair. She knew, despite what her family and society believed, that separating people because of the color of their skin (also called segregation) was wrong. She decided she was going to do something about it when she had the chance.

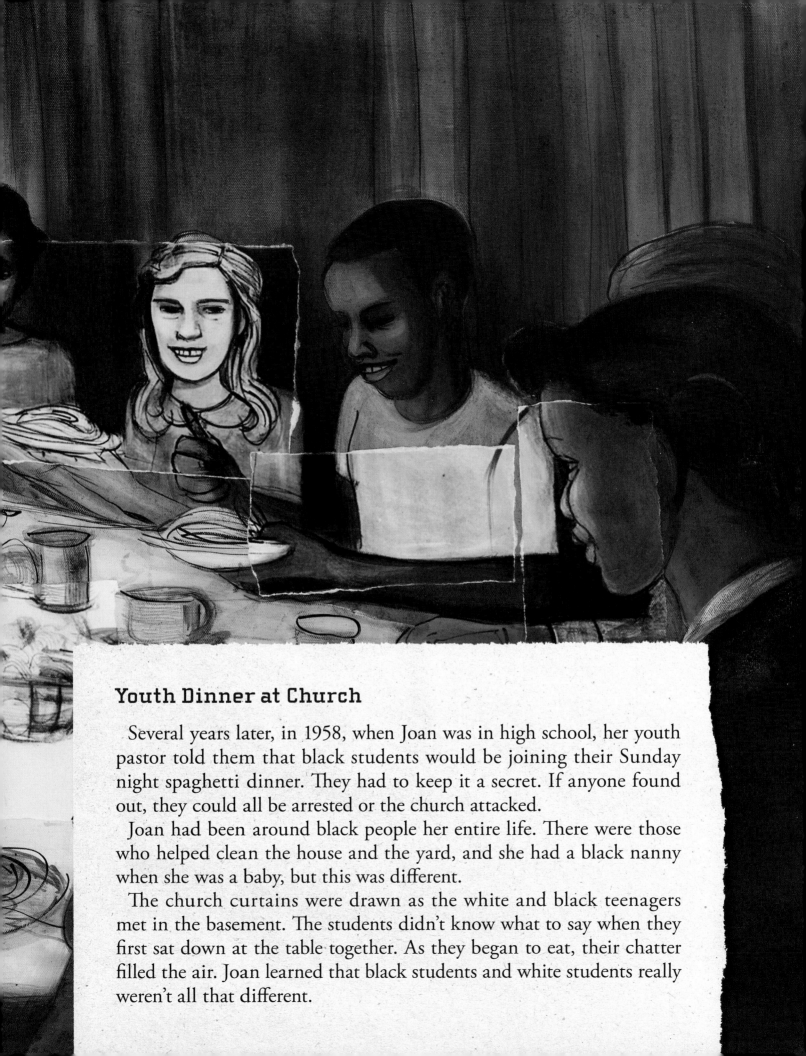

Youth Dinner at Church

Several years later, in 1958, when Joan was in high school, her youth pastor told them that black students would be joining their Sunday night spaghetti dinner. They had to keep it a secret. If anyone found out, they could all be arrested or the church attacked.

Joan had been around black people her entire life. There were those who helped clean the house and the yard, and she had a black nanny when she was a baby, but this was different.

The church curtains were drawn as the white and black teenagers met in the basement. The students didn't know what to say when they first sat down at the table together. As they began to eat, their chatter filled the air. Joan learned that black students and white students really weren't all that different.

From High School to College

Joan graduated from Annandale High in 1959. She wanted to go to college. She didn't want to go to Duke University, but her mother insisted because Duke was a segregated school. She didn't want her daughter to have "colored" classmates or a roommate who was black.

Joan began attending Duke and in the spring was invited to join a demonstration in Durham. A demonstration was a chance for people to get together in public and show they felt strongly about a cause. Joan saw it as a way to try to change people's opinions about segregation, but she knew that if she did, her Georgia family might never speak to her again. She would never be able to go back to the life she knew.

Could she do what was right even if it wasn't easy?

Joan joined the Civil Rights Movement in 1960. Thousands of other people from across the South and the country were standing up for equal rights for everyone.

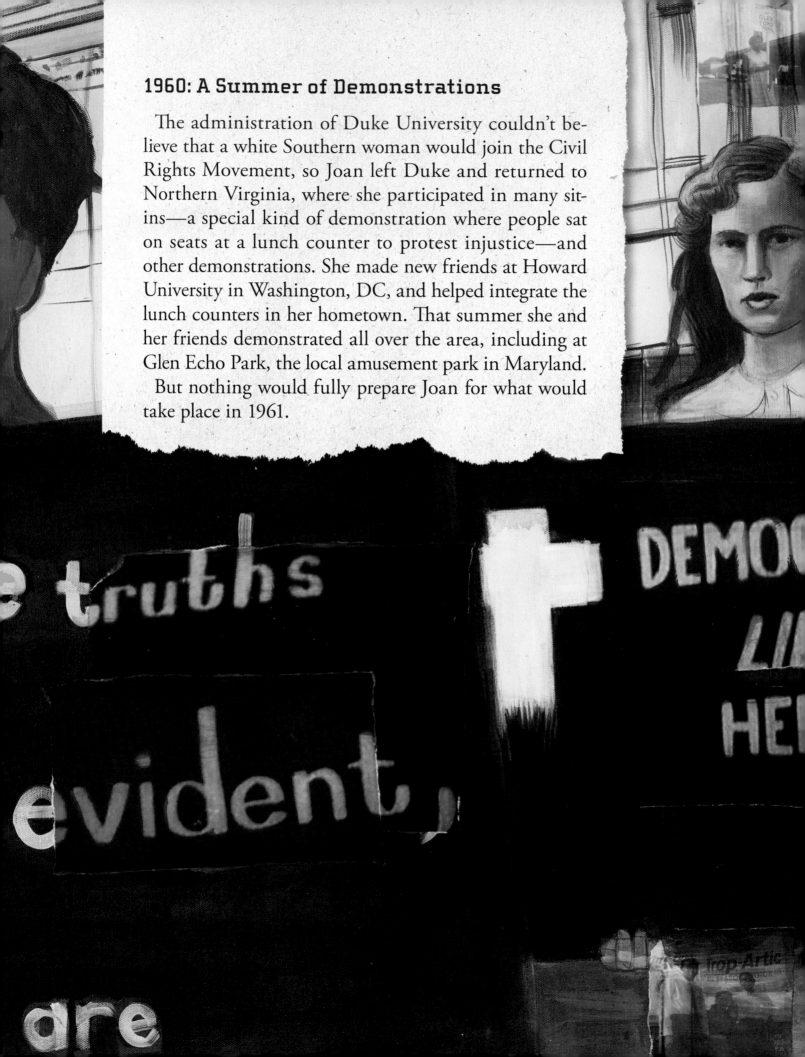

1960: A Summer of Demonstrations

The administration of Duke University couldn't believe that a white Southern woman would join the Civil Rights Movement, so Joan left Duke and returned to Northern Virginia, where she participated in many sit-ins—a special kind of demonstration where people sat on seats at a lunch counter to protest injustice—and other demonstrations. She made new friends at Howard University in Washington, DC, and helped integrate the lunch counters in her hometown. That summer she and her friends demonstrated all over the area, including at Glen Echo Park, the local amusement park in Maryland.

But nothing would fully prepare Joan for what would take place in 1961.

GLEN ECHO
PARK
GLEN ECHO, MARYLAND
PREJUDICE
A COSTLY
COMMODITY
$ $ $
R IS NOT
RTANT
HEART
RACY

Freedom Rides

It was a warm day in May when two interstate passenger buses rolled out of Washington, DC, heading to New Orleans with black and white riders in the seats. It was called the Freedom Rides, and the people on the buses were called Freedom Riders. They wanted to draw attention, in a peaceful way, to unjust segregation in the South. Joan's friend, Hank Thomas, was one of the Riders.

POLICE DEPT.
JACKSON, MISS
20975

Then a photo appeared in the newspaper. Joan was speechless. There was Hank in Anniston, Alabama, standing in front of a bus that was on fire. The Freedom Riders had gotten attention—but not the kind they were hoping for. The Freedom Rides seemed all but over.

Joan and her friends wanted to keep the Freedom Rides going. They flew to New Orleans, took a train to Jackson, Mississippi, and went into the train station together. They were arrested and sent to Hinds County Jail.

Arrested

The county jail was hot and full of other students from all over the country. Joan kept a diary hidden in the hem of her skirt. Life in the county jail became almost routine when rumors started spreading that they would soon be heading to the most notorious prison in America: Parchman.

The old prison farm was deep in the Mississippi Delta, far from the press and from safety. Rumors said that people never returned from Parchman, and the few that did were never quite the same. All Joan and her companions could do was pray as the truck they were transported in drove along the lonely two-lane highway.

At Parchman, the prisoners were separated by race and gender. Joan was taken to cell fourteen in the maximum security unit, where she would spend the next two months, all because she was trying to do what was right.

Fifty years later, she would learn that her cell had been around the corner from the death chamber.

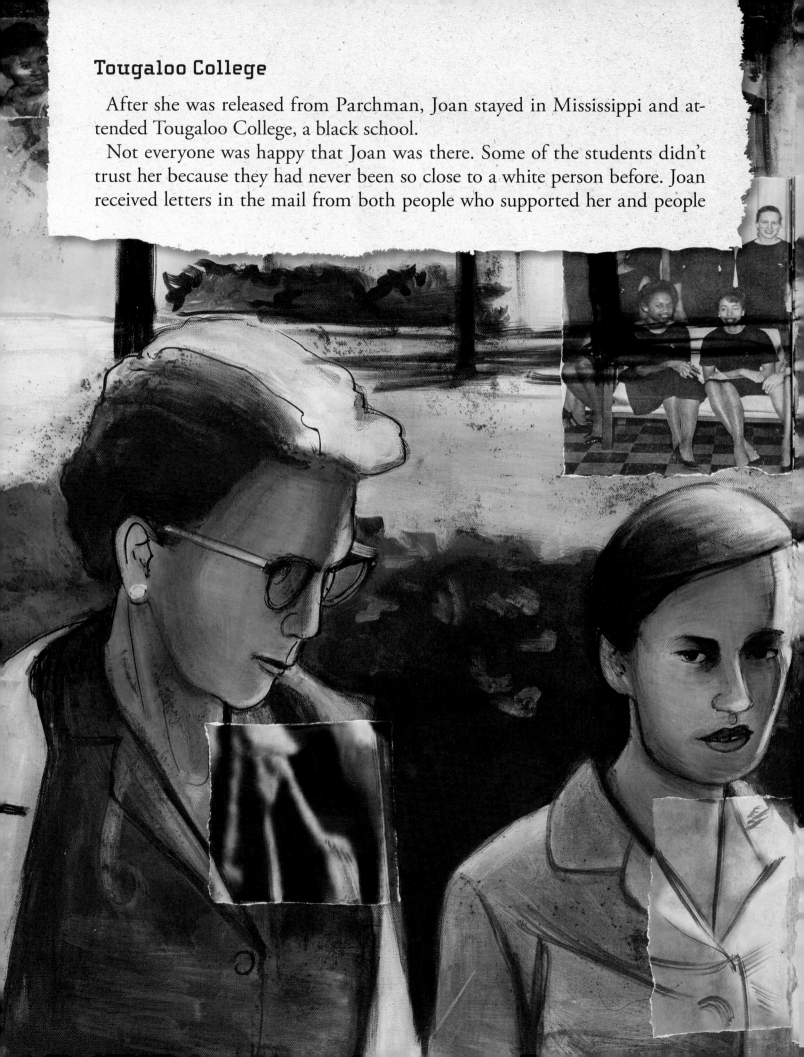

Tougaloo College

After she was released from Parchman, Joan stayed in Mississippi and attended Tougaloo College, a black school.

Not everyone was happy that Joan was there. Some of the students didn't trust her because they had never been so close to a white person before. Joan received letters in the mail from both people who supported her and people

who said she was a traitor. The state of Mississippi even tried to close Tougaloo because of Joan, but they couldn't.

Joan went to classes and studied hard. In 1962, she was invited by her friend, Joyce Ladner, to join the all-black sorority (a student organization for women) Delta Sigma Theta. She even got to meet Dr. Martin Luther King Jr.

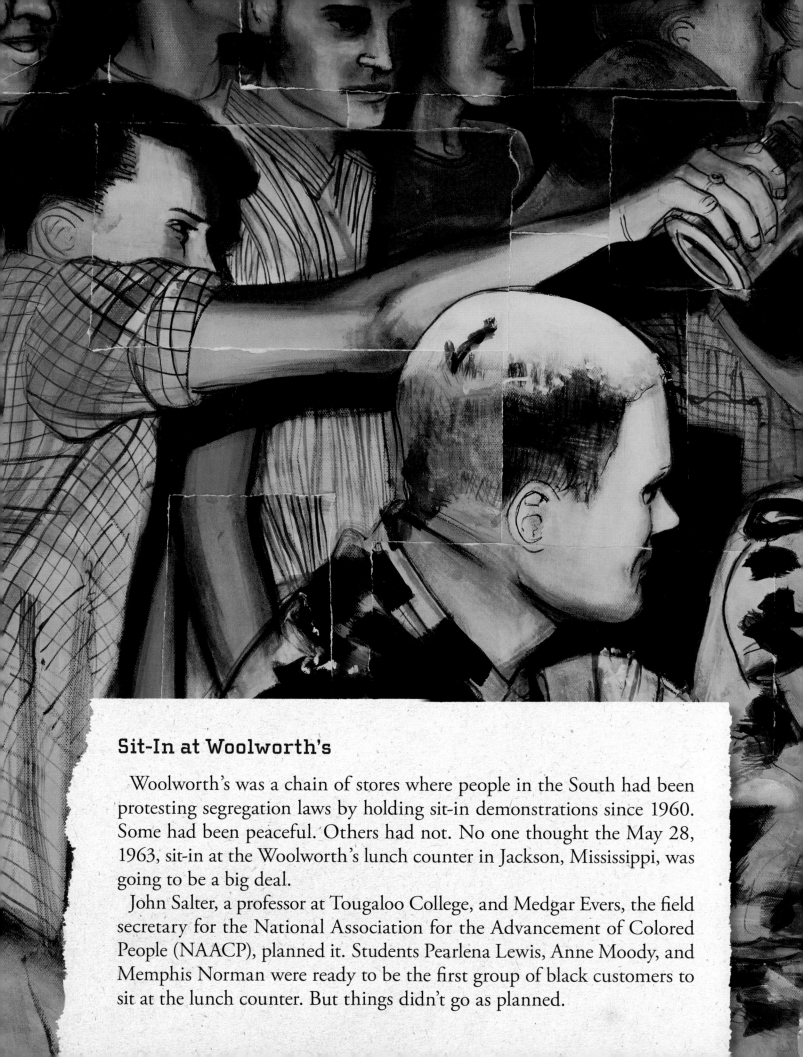

Sit-In at Woolworth's

Woolworth's was a chain of stores where people in the South had been protesting segregation laws by holding sit-in demonstrations since 1960. Some had been peaceful. Others had not. No one thought the May 28, 1963, sit-in at the Woolworth's lunch counter in Jackson, Mississippi, was going to be a big deal.

John Salter, a professor at Tougaloo College, and Medgar Evers, the field secretary for the National Association for the Advancement of Colored People (NAACP), planned it. Students Pearlena Lewis, Anne Moody, and Memphis Norman were ready to be the first group of black customers to sit at the lunch counter. But things didn't go as planned.

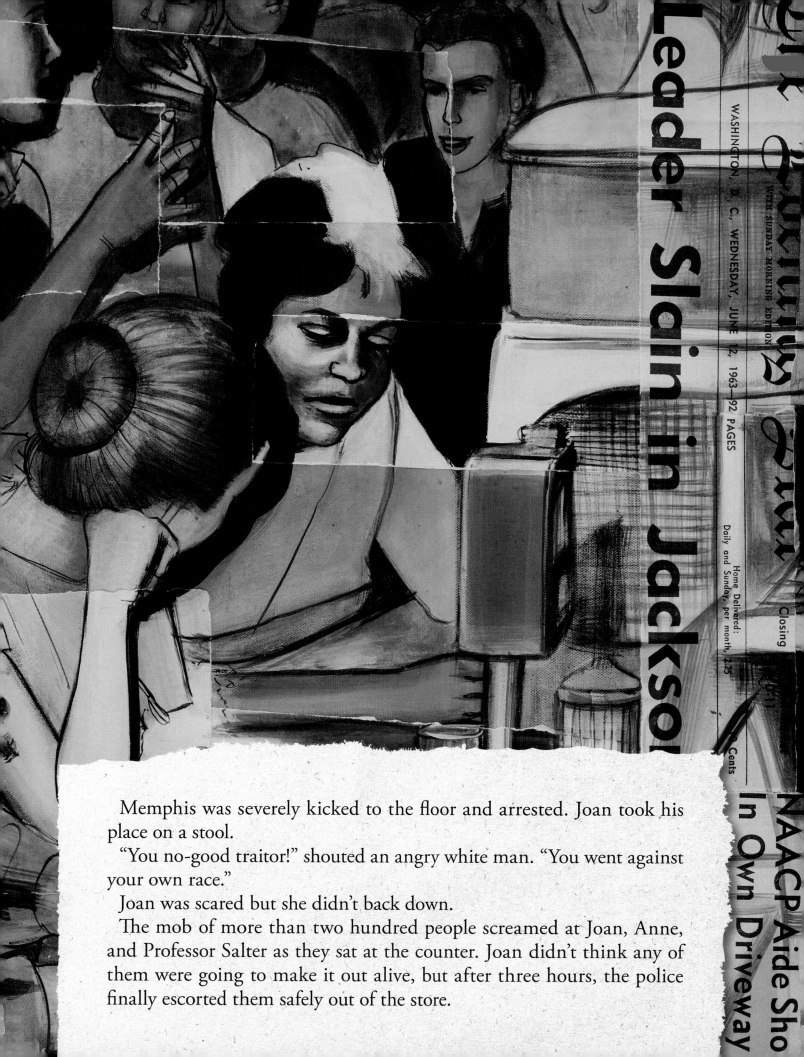

WASHINGTON, D. C., WEDNESDAY, JUNE 12, 1963—92 PAGES

Home Delivered:
Daily and Sunday, per month, 2.25

Closing

Cents

NAACP Aide Sho
In Own Driveway

Memphis was severely kicked to the floor and arrested. Joan took his place on a stool.

"You no-good traitor!" shouted an angry white man. "You went against your own race."

Joan was scared but she didn't back down.

The mob of more than two hundred people screamed at Joan, Anne, and Professor Salter as they sat at the counter. Joan didn't think any of them were going to make it out alive, but after three hours, the police finally escorted them safely out of the store.

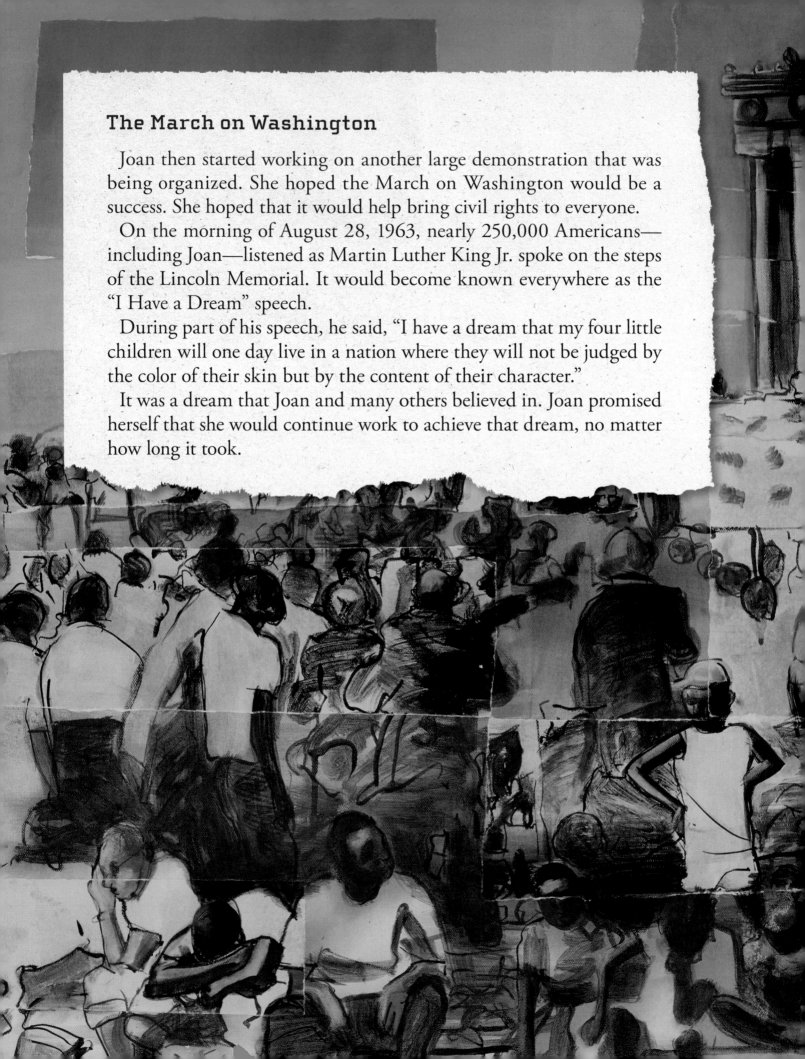

The March on Washington

Joan then started working on another large demonstration that was being organized. She hoped the March on Washington would be a success. She hoped that it would help bring civil rights to everyone.

On the morning of August 28, 1963, nearly 250,000 Americans—including Joan—listened as Martin Luther King Jr. spoke on the steps of the Lincoln Memorial. It would become known everywhere as the "I Have a Dream" speech.

During part of his speech, he said, "I have a dream that my four little children will one day live in a nation where they will not be judged by the color of their skin but by the content of their character."

It was a dream that Joan and many others believed in. Joan promised herself that she would continue work to achieve that dream, no matter how long it took.

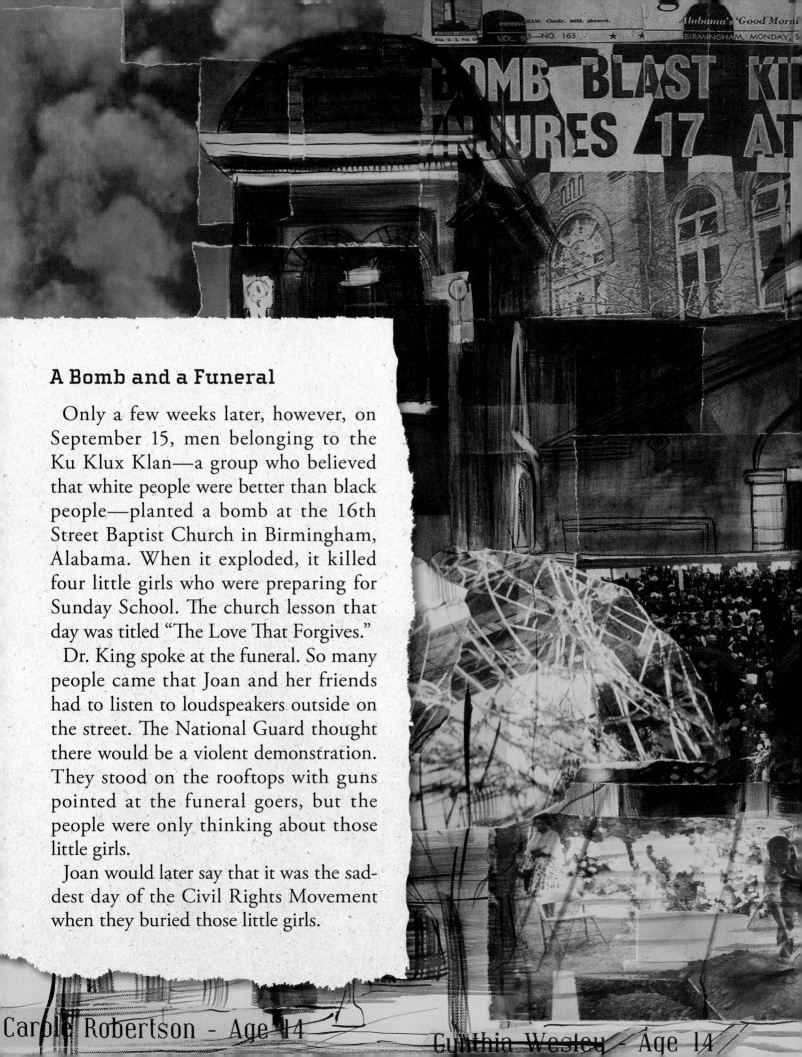

A Bomb and a Funeral

Only a few weeks later, however, on September 15, men belonging to the Ku Klux Klan—a group who believed that white people were better than black people—planted a bomb at the 16th Street Baptist Church in Birmingham, Alabama. When it exploded, it killed four little girls who were preparing for Sunday School. The church lesson that day was titled "The Love That Forgives."

Dr. King spoke at the funeral. So many people came that Joan and her friends had to listen to loudspeakers outside on the street. The National Guard thought there would be a violent demonstration. They stood on the rooftops with guns pointed at the funeral goers, but the people were only thinking about those little girls.

Joan would later say that it was the saddest day of the Civil Rights Movement when they buried those little girls.

Carole Robertson - Age 14   Cynthia Wesley - Age 14

Newspaper ALABAMA: Cloudy, mild, showers. EDITION
TEMBER 16, 1963 22 Pages In Two Sections PRICE FIVE CENTS

LS 4 CHILDREN
CHURCH HERE

Carol Denise McNair - Age 11

Addie Mae Collins - Age 14

The Dangers of Demonstrating

Joan had had brushes with death before. She was chased by angry white men in Jackson. Shots were fired in Arlington and Durham. Police dogs lunged at her in the garage of the jail. When a group of angry men stopped the car she was riding in outside of Canton, Mississippi, in May 1964, she thought her time had come.

The men began beating on the car, trying to get Joan and the others. The mob had already picked out a place to kill them.

She, like several others, was on the Ku Klux Klan's "Most Wanted" list. The Klan believed that killing Joan and the other people in the Civil Rights Movement would stop blacks from seeking the right to vote. Voting meant things would change, and they didn't want things to change.

Freedom Summer

The summer of 1964 was known as "Freedom Summer." People in the Civil Rights Movement wanted to help as many black people as possible register to vote. Some people were attacked or arrested for trying to help. Three of them were killed.

Joan knew the work she and her friends were doing helped give the activists in the Civil Rights Movement the strength to press forward. They knew that good always triumphed over evil. They would succeed, as long as they never quit.

Her Own Family

Joan graduated from Tougaloo College in 1964 and a few years later started a family. She continued to participate in events like the Selma to Montgomery March in 1965 and the Meredith March in 1966. The day President Lyndon B. Johnson said, "And we *shall* overcome," was a powerful moment for Joan. Everyone would now have the opportunity to vote.

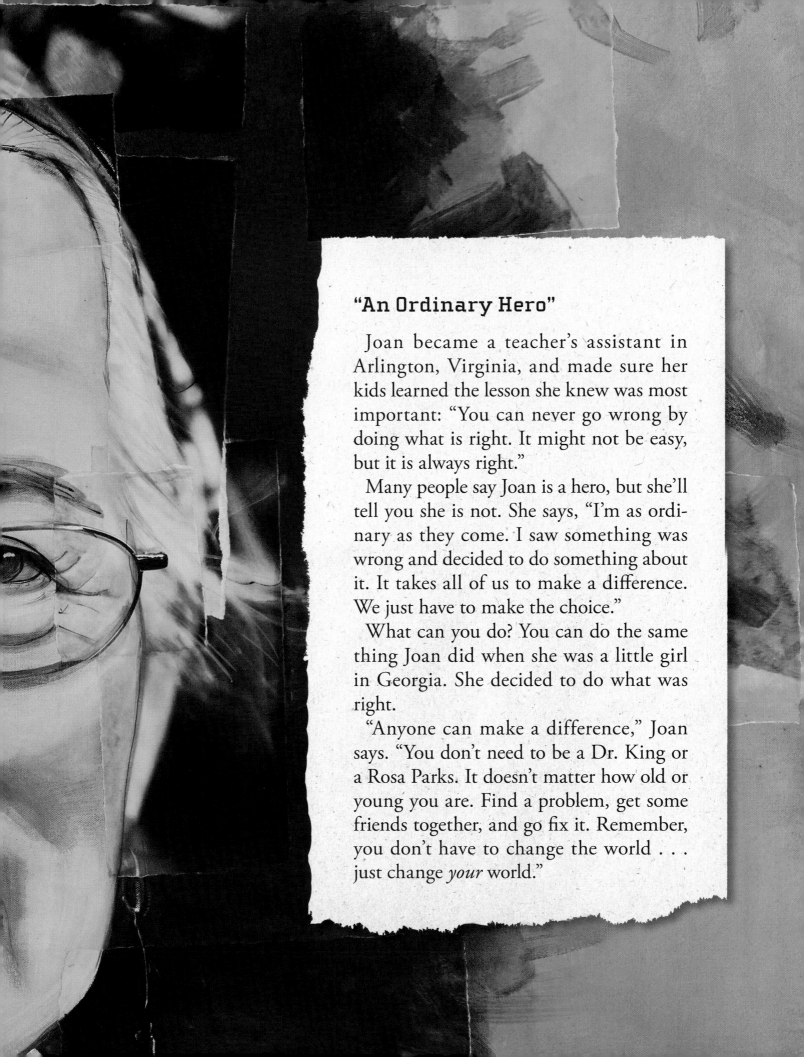

"An Ordinary Hero"

Joan became a teacher's assistant in Arlington, Virginia, and made sure her kids learned the lesson she knew was most important: "You can never go wrong by doing what is right. It might not be easy, but it is always right."

Many people say Joan is a hero, but she'll tell you she is not. She says, "I'm as ordinary as they come. I saw something was wrong and decided to do something about it. It takes all of us to make a difference. We just have to make the choice."

What can you do? You can do the same thing Joan did when she was a little girl in Georgia. She decided to do what was right.

"Anyone can make a difference," Joan says. "You don't need to be a Dr. King or a Rosa Parks. It doesn't matter how old or young you are. Find a problem, get some friends together, and go fix it. Remember, you don't have to change the world . . . just change *your* world."

Civil Rights Timeline

April 15, 1947—Jackie Robinson breaks the "color barrier" and becomes the first black Major League Baseball player.

July 26, 1948—President Truman orders integration of the armed forces.

May 17, 1954—Brown v. Board of Education. Supreme Court rules schools must be integrated. Separate is not equal.

August 28, 1955—Emmett Till, a fourteen-year-old boy, is tortured and killed after being accused of whistling at a white woman.

December 1, 1955—Rosa Parks is arrested for refusing to move to the back of a city bus. Reverend Martin Luther King Jr. leads the Montgomery Bus Boycott.

September 25, 1957—Nine students integrate Central High School in Little Rock, Arkansas.

February 1, 1960—Student lunch counter sit-ins are held throughout the South, beginning in Greensboro, North Carolina.

April 15–17, 1960—Students form the Student Nonviolent Coordinating Committee (SNCC).

November 14, 1960—Ruby Bridges becomes the first black student to attend an all-white elementary school in Louisiana.

May 4, 1961—People participating in the Freedom Rides board buses, trains, and planes to obtain equal treatment in interstate travel (as required by the Supreme Court). Hundreds go to jail.

October 1, 1962—James Meredith becomes the first black student to enroll at the University of Mississippi.

May 2–5, 1963—The Children's Crusade—a march made by hundreds of school students—is attacked by police dogs and fire hoses in Birmingham, Alabama.

May 28, 1963—Sit-in held at a Woolworth's lunch counter in Jackson, Mississippi, is attacked.

June 12, 1963—Civil rights leader Medgar Evers is assassinated in Jackson, Mississippi.

August 27, 1963—Dr. Martin Luther King Jr. leads the March on Washington.

September 15, 1963—Four girls are killed in the bombing of the 16th Street Baptist Church in Birmingham, Alabama.

November 22, 1963—President John F. Kennedy is assassinated in Dallas, Texas.

January 23, 1964—The 24th Amendment abolishes poll taxes.

Summer 1964—Known as "Freedom Summer" in Mississippi. Hundreds of students work for civil rights. Three are killed.

July 2, 1964—Civil Rights Act of 1964 becomes law, outlawing discrimination based on race, color, or religion.

August 24–27, 1964—Fannie Lou Hamer and other members of the Mississippi Freedom Democratic Party demand to be seated at the Democratic National Convention in Atlantic City, New Jersey.

February 21, 1965—Civil Rights leader Malcolm X is assassinated in Harlem, New York.

March 7, 1965—Demonstrators attempt to cross the Edmund Pettus Bridge in Selma, Alabama, but are attacked and beaten by police.

August 6, 1965—President Lyndon B. Johnson signs the Voting Rights Act of 1965 into law.

June 6, 1966—James Meredith begins the March Against Fear from Memphis, Tennessee, to Jackson, Mississippi. He is shot on the second day of the march. Thousands rally to finish the march for him.

April 4, 1968—Civil Rights leader Martin Luther King Jr. is assassinated in Memphis, Tennessee.